To Root, to Toot, to Parachute

What Is a Verb?

To Mary Kate, Jack and Colin —
three 'action' kids
— B P C

To my sister, Margarita
— J P

Verb: A word that shows action or being.

To Root, to Toot, to Parachute

What Is a Verb?

by Brian P Cleary

illustrated by Jenya Prosmitsky

LERNER BOOKS · LONDON · NEW YORK · MINNEAPOLIS

Whether you scale a wall or a fish,

Make a design on a cup or a dish,

4

Take out the rubbish,

or sharpen your knife —

Verbs are a part of your everyday life.

5

To root,
to
toot,

to

parachute,

To play the
saxophone or
flute,

6

To dare,
defend,
descend,
disturb —
If it's an action,
it's a Verb!

7

Verbs are words like sing and dance,

Pray or practise,

preach or prance,

Toss and tumble, jump and jam,

Whine and whisper,

sleep and slam.

9

So are howl, help
and hold,

Whack and stack and pack
and fold,

Fix and finish,

load and lift,

Hurry, scurry, shake and sift.

FLOUR

So take a present,

Send your thanks,

Pull a tooth,
    or pull some pranks,

Blow a bubble,

Sew a sleeve,

You'll use a **Verb** for each of these.

That is fun,

It's been great,

Were you the one who was so late?

Punt or pass or shoot or score,

swim or paddle, pitch or pour,

Jog
or
juggle,

jig or leap,

Verbs can make
you want to sleep.

You can crawl or fall

or pet
your dog,

See a ball game,
be a hog,

Jump and slump and play it cool,

Hunt and hike and bike to school.

19

So pick and fiddle, strum and stroke,

Tease and teeter,

Sob and soak,

Sweep the pavement,
paint the curb,
And know each action
is a Verb!

Have and has belong here too,

Like
'I have

green eyes,

She
has
blue'.

22

Or 'Mandy **has** a
mini mutt'.

These **Verbs** can tell us
who's got what!

23

Verbs tell of ships cruising, dogs snoozing, slime oozing,

They tell of spies spying, guys trying and losing,

of leaves when they're falling, and wind when it's blowing,

The rain when it's raining.

the snow when it's snowing.

They tell us of dogs
that are barking or sleeping,

BEEP
BEEP

Of cars that are racing,
or merely beep-beeping,

Of planes that
are flying,

and trains choo-choo-chooing,

Aunt Edna
'Oh-Hi-ing',

and Mum
'Toodle-ooing' —

27

Of corn that is popping,

and singers doo-Wopping,

of folks that are sweeping,

and afterwards, mopping,

So, whether it's
dangerous,
dull or superb,

Each sentence, you see,
simply must have a **Verb!**

VERB POWER

VERBS ARE COOL

ABOUT THE AUTHOR & ILLUSTRATOR

BRIAN P CLEARY is the author of the best-selling Words Are CATegorical™ series as well as the Math is CATegorical™ series, Peanut Butter and Jellyfishes: A Very Silly Alphabet Book, Rainbow Soup: Adventures in Poetry, and Rhyme & PUNishment: Adventures in Wordplay. Mr Cleary lives in Cleveland, USA.

JENYA PROSMITSKY grew up and studied art in Chisinau, Moldova, and lives in Minneapolis, USA. Her two cats, Henry and Freddy, were vital to her illustrations for this book.

Text copyright © 2001 by Lerner Publishing Group, Inc.

First published in the United States of America in 2001

First published in the United Kingdom in 2009 by
Lerner Books,
Dalton House,
60 Windsor Avenue,
London SW19 2RR

Website address: www.lernerbooks.co.uk

This edition was updated and edited for UK publication by Discovery Books Ltd.,
Unit 3, 37 Watling Street, Leintwardine, Shropshire, SY7 0LW

British Library Cataloguing in Publication Data

Cleary, Brian P., 1959-
To root, to toot, to parachute : what is a verb?. – 2nd ed. –
(Words are categorical)
1. English language – Verb – Juvenile poetry
I. Title
425.6

ISBN-13: 978 0 7613 4272 4

Printed in China